The Sentence.

The Sentence.

poems   MORRI CREECH

Louisiana State University Press
Baton Rouge

Published by Louisiana State University Press
lsupress.org

LSU Press Paperback Original

Designer: Barbara Neely Bourgoyne
Typeface: FreightText Pro

Library of Congress Cataloging-in-Publication Data
Names: Creech, Morri, 1970– author.
Title: The sentence : poems / Morri Creech.
Other titles: Sentence (Compilation)
Description: Baton Rouge : Louisiana State University Press, [2023]
Identifiers: LCCN 2022058679 (print) | LCCN 2022058680 (ebook) | ISBN
    978-0-8071-8015-0 (paperback) | ISBN 978-0-8071-8034-1 (pdf) | ISBN
    978-0-8071-8033-4 (epub)
Subjects: LCSH: Mortality—Poetry. | LCGFT: Poetry.
Classification: LCC PS3603.R44 S46 2023 (print) | LCC PS3603.R44 (ebook) |
    DDC 811/.6—dc23/eng/20230418
LC record available at https://lccn.loc.gov/2022058679
LC ebook record available at https://lccn.loc.gov/2022058680

for Sarah, Hattie, and Miriam

CONTENTS

The Sentence.

Inscription

The fire of evening went out spark by spark;
we dream the days and wake up to the dark.

I.

The Sentence

Death is a nagging grit, that grain I keep
worrying furiously into the pearl of art—

how is that for an opening sentence? It is,
in fact, the closing sentence, the Omega

toward which the Alpha
stumbles whenever one says the alphabet.

In the ramifying narrative of syntax
the subject makes its pilgrimage (though bound

up in the cursive and recursive loops,
the digressions constituting the long skein

that tangles all the meanings) to the full
stop, which sentences everyone in time.

Word after word, linked like a string of pearls.
The theme of that lucid sentence? A belief

the sentence will not end, since it is not
being—indeed it must not be—

spoken by me alone: each time we speak
a dead man's words, his lips move in the grave.

Shadow

He got up. It was there. And it was growing
from much the same place it had been before.
It had followed him to sleep without his knowing
and, once he rose, had crept up to the door.

In much the same place it had been before
it skulked behind him while he brushed his teeth.
And when he turned it crept up to the door,
a stain that seemed to spread from underneath

the parted curtains. While he brushed his teeth
he thought of all he'd come to know of it.
Which wasn't much. It spread from underneath
his being anywhere the rooms were lit:

the one thing that he'd come to know of it.
Sometimes it stretched out next to him, a double
that kept close to him when the room was lit
or waited for him in the dark like trouble.

Somehow it seemed unsettling, like a double
exposure, or the outline of the moon—
not waiting for him in the dark like trouble
but giving rise to doubts he felt at noon,

disturbing as the outline of the moon.
For a while he simply put it from his mind.
Still, though, he felt it nagging him at noon,
an existential wake he trailed behind

him. He tried hard to put it from his mind.
He focused on his work, his kids, his wife,
as though he didn't trail its wake behind
the half of him he'd come to call "my life,"

the part that had a job, three kids, a wife,
and, here and there, a good time with his friends.
This was the half he'd come to call his life;
the other kept pursuing its own ends.

On nights when he was out late with his friends
it opened beneath the streetlamp like a rose
and seemed to be pursuing other ends;
where does it go, he thought, *when my eyes close?*

It opened beneath the streetlamp like a rose
and followed him to sleep without his knowing.
What happens to it after my eyes close?
The question troubled him. And it kept growing.

Grievance

I am tired of having a name.
Every time I wake
it grinds its teeth
like the gears of a moving van,
and it smells of soot,
like the sweat of being a man,
and it weighs like a stone
I carry for no one's sake.

In the courthouse it echoes
down the long corridors,
and it creaks in the bedsprings
of cheap rooms, and it croons in bars;
it whistles up to the gaps
between the stars
and down to the truck stop
bathroom's piss-stained floors.

I have betrayed it to the dark
when there was no one to blame
and whispered it seductively
into the ear of danger.
But I am tired, and I want
to be done with it for good.

I will give it up. I will answer
to nothing. I will be
a stranger. I will put on the silence
like an executioner's hood.
Here it is, poor neck
squirming on the block: my name.

Suit

El traje que vestí mañana . . .
—César Vallejo

The suit I wore tomorrow
lies folded beneath the clock.

Its sleeves are full of shadows.
The pearls of its buttons shine.

Though I cannot wear it now,
I wait for the chill of silk

and the wings of herringbone
to make space for my body;

I wait to feel the present
raise anchor again slowly

from the dark estuaries
of pockets and shirt collars

to drift in bottomless hours.
The thin pleats of the trousers

lie sharp as a horizon;
the hems bound their emptiness;

but it is always later.
Each time I put on the suit

I fabricate a way past
the barbarous afternoons

of blue, desolate windows,
the arias of sirens,

and sail on, trailing the spume
of the minutes in my wake.

When I wear it tomorrow,
let my backward shadow fall

on the one who waits here now,
in this ill-fitting moment,

awaiting his change of clothes.
After all the threads have frayed,

let there be the kiss of silk
in the soiled laundry of days.

Mirrors

One afternoon when snow fell on the lawns
and winter light grew thinner in the trees,
he stood in his grandmother's beauty parlor
and, over his shoulder, trained a handheld mirror
at the mirror behind him. The wall clock was silent.
The domes of the big hair dryers gathered dust.
What he saw both entertained and startled him:
his head and face repeated in a corridor
of bizarre, ever-shrinking iterations,
a duplicate geometry of selves,
each one of them turned toward its opposite
in infinitely receding parallels.
It confirmed his suspicions: he was himself,
of course, but he was other people, too,
the strangers that he knew he didn't know
—the ones whose backs were always turned to him—
and those whom he was sure he recognized:
the boy in the beauty parlor and the one
who looked out at rough shadows on the sea;
the kid who snickered while he took communion
and the other one who daydreamed in his room—
as well as all of those he knew from moods
whose vagaries had made him speculate
about the winds behind their random weather.
Who was it that kept staring at him now?
He watched this boy whom he had studied closely
in endless ramifications in the glass,
and mused in his own prism of reflection
while the second hand advanced on the clock:
everyone he was was sunk in the mirror,
myriads of himself diminishing
farther and farther toward the edge of vision,
until, anonymous, they disappeared.

Search

I'm the new catalog of creation.
I'm the data from Rome to Riyadh.
I'm the shrine of late-night masturbation.
I'm the postmodern version of God.

For each dexterous click of the fingers
I'm a smart algorithm grown wise.
I appeal to both left- and right-wingers.
I can see behind every disguise.

I'm a cursor just waiting to tell you
the thing that you most want to know.
I can show you the blueprints to Bellevue.
I can help you make plenty of dough.

Do your night sweats mean you have cancer?
Are you worried that mole has changed shape?
For each question I have the right answer.
For each mousetrap I have an escape.

Here's a formula for nuclear fission
and directions for baking a cake.
Here's how to make a decision
when it's late and you're still wide awake.

I can help you sustain an erection.
I know all your secrets by heart.
I can influence a public election
and interpret your medical chart.

I'll soothe you when you feel defeated.
Believe me. Just pick up the phone.
I'll tell you all you've ever needed.
I'll tell you your life is your own.

House of Correction

NIGHTFALL

Once the witches were burned and the shopkeepers swept the ashes from the street, we went inside for supper. Smoke hung in the trees like damp shirts on the line. The evening light kept making its slow concessions. At the table, we dragged our forks across our empty plates and watched the weather change from the open window. And what was that ragged noise the blackbirds made, preening themselves in the field under a snatch of cloud? What about that faint, steady drip at the backyard spigot? Mother leaned close in her fever chair, whispering to us as though the dark were listening.

CALVARY

The thief on the cross stole a glance in our direction. It was a feast day, for what saint I forget. There were jugglers and bears chained to stakes and prostitutes shaking their bangles at the foot of the hill. When the thief raised his head, they all clapped; when he slumped, they grew bored. Children were playing jacks with the teeth of the dead. The thief looked down at them grimly. One boy, I remember, scooped up nine silver crowns before the ball bounced in the dust.

DREAM WORK

The hangman's nightmares were never terrible enough. Once, war, famine, and pestilence had been his evening delights, but these happened less and less as he got older. He had to make do with cats flayed in lamplight, the tired anguish of thumbscrews, a few furtive crucifixions. The pleasures of pain seemed nearly over. He could do nothing now but endure night's insipid disappointments, again and again fitting his neck into the slender noose of sleep.

SALVATION

In the house of correction, all the maimed saints work overtime. They sweep and mop the floors, extract confessions, and take turns flipping the switch on the electric chair. One sports a scalp tattoo of Jesus weeping, another a sleeve of the mortal world in flames. They punch their timecards like anybody else. It's hard, thankless work. They sleep poorly every night, tossing on their mattresses of straw, dreaming of salvation. A stranger in heaven loves them all.

TAROT

The town psychic, busy at her cards, didn't notice the moment when the future turned into the present. "Here is the wheel on which you will be broken," she said, and flashed her cheap rings at us while she cut the deck. But the present already loomed at the windowsill. We saw cities burning on the plain, ashes in the wells, and refugees with no passports stranded in the country of the mad. Then slowly the fires went out. The present was over. We pointed to the ruins in the distance. When she drew her next card, all that we had seen—the shattered stores and houses, the crumbling towers, everything—dissolved into a thin, bitter smoke.

Mileage

The car mechanic's counting out his bills
behind the E-Z Mart at one a.m.;
he'll toss rocks at beer bottles just for thrills
until his dealer comes, it's fine with him.

He draws in a deep breath and sees the light
swerve from the highway, puzzling the back wall
he leans against just to keep out of sight—
a quarter bag and some fentanyl, that's all.

His phone vibrates again though nothing's wrong.
For two years he's been living in a trailer
with a girl who works at Publix. They get along
even if sometimes she says he's a failure—

what can he say to that? Sure. He lives cheap.
They'll fight until she forces a decision,
then roll around on the couch. Once she's asleep
he'll take a dose and watch some television.

At night he dreams of cylinders and sprockets,
the trucks and cars too busted up to fix;
startled awake, eyes aching in their sockets,
he'll watch the clock hands grope their way to six.

A car pulls up, but he can see it's not
his hookup. Just kids with nothing else to do
but drink a six-pack in the parking lot
before they head out to the lake to screw.

He had his share of mischief, too, Lord knows.
The girls don't eye him in the check-out aisle
much anymore, the ones with painted toes.
A few years back, at least, they used to smile.

The boys can see the grease that stains his hands;
they all think, damn, who wants to work that hard?
He spends the day beneath their dads' sedans
while they play tackle football in the yard.

Chasing a football blew out both his knees
and broke his wrist. That was three years ago.
Customers say, "Go Stags," and toss their keys,
then look at him real close as if they know.

A text says no one's coming. The BP sign
flickers over the pumps, and though it's half
past two now, and he's tired, he's feeling fine
enough to think that it's a bust, and laugh.

And, anyway, it's good to be alone
with the gas fumes and blinking traffic light
and fifteen missed calls lighting up his phone.
Later, he thinks, once he and his girl fight,

and once she falls asleep on his left arm,
he'll stare at the pattern on the ceiling tile
and wait to hear the clock sound its alarm
while the night's odometer counts one more mile.

Time

PAST

This sonnet you once wrote is finished now.
Hospital bracelet on the moment's wrist,
item not found on the Official List—
I am the snicker when you take your bow.

Call me the whisper in the wings, the baize
on which the dice get thrown, the backward look.
I'm the initials in the ledger book,
the lengthening sentence you worry phrase by phrase.

My accusations glare from every mirror.
I know you well and answer to your name.
Each time you smile, my wrinkles show up clearer;

each time you break an oath, I take the blame.
And though you don't mistake me for a friend,
trust me: I'm all you'll think of at the end.

PRESENT

What is this threshold Buddha once grew wise on
watching a dust mote balance on the light;
sill over which the swallow floats midflight,
as lean and measureless as the horizon?

What am I—swimmer caught between a shore
he can't return to and one he can't quite reach,
who makes for a retreating stretch of beach
and ends, with each stroke, where he was before?

Arrow that never finds its target, flower
dying into bloom, door that doesn't close,
you change the instant that I say *you are.*

How is it that my life both stays and goes?
Shade of the gnomon inches toward the hour.
Your shutter stills each motion to a pose.

FUTURE

I will be good. I will behave next time.
I will be more discerning when I choose.
I will swear off the gambling and the booze
and make a full confession of my crime.

I will repair the foundation brick by brick
to keep my cut-price Babel from collapse.
I will step clear of all tripwires and traps.
I will work hard and not be such a prick.

And won't things be much different tomorrow?
And won't I nose the trough to get my fill?
And won't I be relieved of every sorrow?

And won't there be some cash left in the till?
So everyone thinks they have time to borrow,
whispering down to the last: *I will, I will.*

House Fire at the Sea

Neither was sure what drew them toward the sand
to watch the fire. Along the beach, the smoke
had plumed across the roofs that night to wake
them in their own house farther up the strand.

They'd walked a quarter mile to see it burn,
while a few curious strangers tagged along
and the surf broke like there was nothing wrong,
like the house fire was none of its concern.

No one could tell what started it. The neighbors
trailing their bathrobes had each made a guess,
but no one knew or no one would confess.
Beyond, the firemen still performed their labors.

The woman looked to sea and watched how flame
reflected on the breaker's cresting rim,
glimmered past the tideline, then grew dim.
With every wave the fire shone much the same.

The man had turned his back to her. He spoke
to someone out of view, but she could hear
his voice and see his hands quick in the air
either making a point or fanning away the smoke.

How strange, she thought, to see a fire so close
to the one element that could have tamed it.
"The place went up before the owners named it,"
she heard the man declare as the flames rose.

They'd stayed in a house like this when they first met.
Three floors and a verandah. Not so far
from the boardwalk, which had a daiquiri bar,
where they drank after swimming, hair still wet.

Later on they would make love, talk, or read—
the sea had been the source of all they shared.
And if they had been careless, no one cared;
she'd never felt so captive or so freed.

The fire deepened the shadows where he stood.
He looked the same, as far as she could tell.
And if some things had passed between them? Well.
Talking about them now would do no good.

The firemen climbed their ladders in the dark,
but the house was empty. No one had been there.
All that the rest of them could do was stare.
The thick smoke hid the moon but left no mark.

Near Murrell's Inlet

The flatteries of the surf conspire to make
a stammering innuendo in the reeds.
The sun, splintered by the spume's refractions,
sinks toward the west where it will disappear
in a violet streak above the evening dunes,
like mind considering the defeat of mind.
A cormorant in the distance breaks the surface
to wrestle a mullet from the sullen depths
farther below which no light penetrates.
As much as the theorems and hypotheses
that trouble sleep, as much as love or God
or the errant rhetoric of the passions,
as much as the tired flirtations of moon and cloud,
it is kinship to those depths one chiefly thinks of,
dark like the inward concave of the skull
and fathomless as a notion's origin,
a place that nothing reaches, where the prinks
of sunlight shrink like a contracting pupil
into a dimming and entropic Zen
that refines every sense to senselessness,
even the thought that drowns in thought itself . . .
    The mind at last, exhausted, surfaces
to what it can confirm, the blues, the bronzes,
the contours and insinuations of the real
where there is so much motion, shape, design
—the rinse and symmetry of wave on wave
unvexed by the struts and vagrancies of sandpipers,
spilling over into a still tide pool
in which a couple of bathers are parading—
that all the mind can do is add its palette
to the streaks and the extravagant daubs of color,
making a makeshift paradigm of dunes
and clouds and sea, the sun's pernicious eye,
each green idea buoyed over the mindless deep.

Prayer

Pith of the rendezvous that looms ahead,
   mirror in which I do not see my face,
groom at the chapel waiting, still unwed,
   voice on the phone impossible to trace,
   I know the sea's taste and the smell of rain,
I've heard the magpies skimming the blue trees
    without you there to confess or to explain
how all things go back to the dark again
   despite a few memorable ecstasies,
    seeming, to no one, never to have been.

Condition

At night in the emergency room, beneath the flicker of fluorescent lights, a man sits in a plastic chair and waits. He hears the entrance door open and close behind him, and the faint squeak of orthopedic shoes. The man squints at the forms, then fills out the column of empty boxes. What symptoms does he have? He has a family and a mortgage. A tire swing's dead weight hanging from the oak tree in his yard. He has occasional bouts of clarity followed by days of deep, persistent doubt. A woman in the seat across from him riffles the pages of a magazine. The man asks what condition brought her there. "Something is killing me," she says; "whatever it is, I've had it since I was a child." Another man chimes in, "I get night sweats thinking about the dawn. I lie awake, propped on a pillow, chewing my nails in dread." Others in the room stare at their phone screens or down at their shoes. The hands spin slowly on the clock above them. Maybe I should just leave, the man thinks; maybe I'm not really sick at all. He presses his hand to his forehead. "There's no use trying to diagnose yourself," the woman whispers, looking pale and shaken. "All you can do is wait, like everyone, until the night nurse comes with her chart and calls your name."

Witness

Your uncles leave you waiting by the shoulder
while they hunt deer in the woods in winter snow.
You've paced the blacktop's edge an hour or so.
The sun's just halfway up. It's getting colder.

Their orange jackets flash between the pines.
Beagles are on the scent to flush the buck
out toward the highway past the pickup truck,
where the men will shoot it on the yellow lines.

The morning sky snags in your memory—
stars that glint like mica flecks on the blue
background a quarter moon is showing through,
above the route from Cross to Elloree.

You hear wheels in the distance, and you think,
what if a deer comes bounding toward the road?
Just then the car appears like time has slowed:
a Pontiac Firebird slipping on the brink

of the iced bridge that spans Jim Cumbee's creek,
its chainless tires chewing the roadside gravel.
A tree snaps like a judge slamming a gavel,
and you can see the skid marks where they streak

maybe ten feet away from where you stand,
the tire tracks aiming toward the distant trees
and the car flipped over, leaking antifreeze.
Out of the windshield juts a woman's hand.

You scramble closer to the wreck and see
she's still as starlight. Pinned there. She can't move.
Somewhere a gear is clicking in its groove.
The radio plays Tom Petty's "Refugee."

You listen for her breath, but it gets slower.
The way the glass-chips in the snow are lit
seems beautiful, a fact you don't admit.
It's dark inside. You can't tell if you know her.

And that's when it capers into the road. The deer.
It stands there a minute, startled. Then it runs
before the men come shouting with their guns.
Just how long you stand watching isn't clear.

Years from now when you recall this morning
it won't be a blur of metal you think of first,
how the Firebird veered off the road, then burst
into the scrim of pine trees without warning,

not the cold, or what song the radio had on—
it won't even be the dead girl they pulled out
of a strew of glass. No. You'll think about
the deer. How it glanced up at you. And was gone.

II.

The Sentence

Osip Mandelstam, transit camp near
Vladivostok, December 1938

1.

Nothing beyond the eastern wire.
A guard stands posted on the tower.

Under each swaying stem of fire
the flakes of ash betray the hour.

Your breath plumes in the winter air,
drifting between the window grates.

Any decent hunger you could bear
lies far outside the prison gates.

Those dreams of wine and caviar
and sweet, clear wells in Novgorod

seem distant as a dying star,
behind which broods an absent God.

2.

You're nearly done with poetry—
pages you hid, once, in your sleeves.

With each dull bureaucrat's decree
a widow in the province grieves.

Your widow (in a bit more time)
combs each page you thought to save,

burying every scrap of rhyme
to keep you from an open grave.

And here you are. The moon is cold.
It follows you most every night.

Iced puddles make it glint like gold
in lines you labor to get right.

3.

Above the troops on night detail
the stars—salt on an ax blade—burn.

You try to stand but you're too frail.
A rifle cracks. It's not your turn.

The goldfinch chirping in your head
swivels his neck and looks both ways

(lines you once crammed beneath the bed
to keep from some official's gaze).

He hops around from thought to thought
and settles on an empty page.

You wrote the words that got you caught.
The winter goldfinch pecks his cage.

4.

In Petersburg you'll find her soon,
your wife. Not how you hoped to meet.

Behind the wire it's almost noon.
Your shoes are crumbling from your feet.

The sickness transport makes you ride
with twenty men laid hip to hip,

but with no Virgil for a guide.
You feel your mind begin to slip.

And Petersburg seems far away,
a wrong address, some name you heard,

a dream that you still won't betray.
You find your way there word for word.

5.

The cockroach crawling Stalin's lip
has found its way into your bowl.

You lift it out, then take a sip.
Outside, armed soldiers walk patrol.

The poems, a charge that nothing clears,
are sealed up in the mouths of friends;

long after fate has closed her shears
they'll quote them to the April winds.

But now the snow begins to fall
and there's not much time left for you.

It's getting late. Nothing is all.
A black thread ravels from its clew.

6.

Your lips are moving in the grave
but you're not dead. The words are yours.

And what else is there left to save?
The wind slips underneath the doors

and through holes in your threadbare coat.
Icicles hang from razor wire

like footnotes to those lines you wrote,
against which all the stars conspire.

Listen. It's snowing. Close your eyes.
Take with you all they couldn't take.

One poem outlasts a thousand lies.
Your words survive. But you won't wake.

Triumph of the New

The gallows and the galleries were there.
Bartenders raised their hazel drams at dawn.
No voices broke the silence of the square.
The torturer smiled and put her lipstick on.

Bartenders raised their hazel drams at dawn
to toast the manifesto up in flames.
The torturer smiled and put her lipstick on,
and the inspector wrote down all the names.

To acknowledge the manifesto up in flames,
the generals lifted their hands in salute.
An investigator wrote down all the names.
The local hangman wore his leather suit.

The generals finished making their salute
since there was nothing left for them to do.
The local hangman, wearing his leather suit,
said to the cameras, "Behold the New,

which, inevitable, governs all we do.
It holds the past to blame for everything
(so do not blame the triumph of the New).
At noon, when fields are fresh, the bells will ring

to say the past's to blame for everything.
We curse the old man's cartwheel on the hill.
At noon, when fields are fresh and the bells ring,
we'll seek the darkness out, and, lovely still,

curse the old man's cartwheel on the hill."
The Tarot lady, reading her cards in braille,
lay down in the shadows, completely still,
and prayed to the random mercies of the hail.

The Tarot lady read her cards in braille.
The inquisitor kept his face behind a mask,
oblivious to the mercies of the hail,
and fixed his mind on finishing his task.

The inquisitor kept his face behind a mask
and, pacing the interrogation room,
fixed his mind on finishing his task.
A bride informed on her arrested groom.

Doctors pronounced the interrogation room
"necessary." (Everyone tells a lie.)
A bride informed on her arrested groom,
then slipped away as through a needle's eye.

Because, in the end, everyone tells a lie,
the dead lay buried near the city gates.
None of them quite fit through the needle's eye.
Theirs was only one of many fates.

The dead lay buried near the city gates.
The gallows and the galleries were there.
Though theirs was only one of many fates,
No voices broke the silence of the square.

If Shakespeare

Shakespeare's sister took the stones from her pockets and climbed out of the river. She wrung her long hair dry and put on the kettle for tea. In the study she opened the books she didn't write; then sat at the desk, lifted a quill, and, in a patient script, wrote nothing down. It was the late sixteenth century. Men brawled in taverns for laurel crowns. And what did she have to say? She was sure that she knew. There were too many words already and none of them hers. Shakespeare's sister scratched her name into the wall with a butter knife. As she paced the floor alone, her thoughts were like starlings at the edge of a winter field, hunting for grass seed. And when she spoke, the sound was like wind tangled in rich curtains, an echo muffled by blank walls, while, in the next room, the kettle on the stove began to sing.

Burning the Leaves

Dad wheelbarrows the leaves into the ditch.
November, and the ground is tinged with frost,
air heavy with smoke, the autumn colors rich.
He squints at the camera, looking vaguely lost.
Mom leans against the handle of her rake
next to the trailer, thinking God knows what,
as though the day were just some big mistake.
A marriage and prim lawn are what she's got,
plus a kid who whizzes by on roller skates,
small at the road's edge but there all the same.
She looks at something far away and waits.
The years crowd in around the picture frame.
The dead leaves at her feet keep piling higher
and, in the background, you can see the fire.

The Trial

Jemand mußte Josef K. verleumdet haben . . .
—Franz Kafka

INSOMNIA

It was just after midnight when Joseph K. awoke, and he suspected at once that his phone had illuminated with some new message about his case. But it lay mute on the nightstand table where he had left it, its screen a mirror in which, he hesitated to think, the darkness could see itself. In bed he held his breath, imagining dust settle on the brass mantelpiece clock and the neat row of ironed shirts in his closet. Down the hall he could hear the refrigerator's hum, a low drone that only made the interstitial silences more distressing. Headlights in the window projected their lunar pallor across the wall, swerving slowly at first and then vanishing. Most perplexing was that every time he closed his eyes, he saw Lady Justice tucked under his comforter, blindfolded and sunk in a profound sleep, her scales weighing his most intimate possessions: balanced in the left pan were his comb and toothbrush, in the right his razor and shoes. K. yawned. Soon he would have to get up and prepare his defense. Arm under his pillow, he kept one eye open, thinking of everything he may or may not have done, and watched a white spider dangle its gallows thread from the ceiling.

AN EXCURSION

Joseph K., accompanied by a colleague from work, drove his small yellow sedan to the coast. The beach sprawled flat and empty before them, with clouds like confections and no other noise than the surf and a few pale birds maundering down the strand. K. was about to spread a picnic blanket and weight the corners with his shoes, when his colleague stripped off his speedo, twirling it high above his head, and dashed into the water, where he instantly disappeared. K. scanned the breakers, the restless water, the sun's dazzling refractions, and wondered where he could have gone. A strong swimmer, had he merely swum beyond the tideline, soon to return? Or had an undertow pulled him down at once? K. didn't know. He was sure an accident on holiday would be construed as evidence. It occurred to K. that he should dive in after him; but the notion seemed absurd. Distracted by the distant calm, the clouds, and the sandpipers strutting leisurely in the shallows, K. decided that he would wait, just as he had become accustomed to doing. The sky overhead was immense. The sand kept going for miles in either direction. Surely, he thought to himself, any minute now, something will happen.

ALTERATIONS

K. arose, dressed, and walked down the avenue past rows of linden trees and past the municipal park (the beaks of its three haggard drakes were buried in their reflections) to the tailor's little shop on the adjacent street. The bell jangled briefly and the heavy door swung closed behind him. No one greeted him there except for the tailor's dummies, which seemed to be regarding him though they had no heads. At last the old tailor climbed out from beneath the counter. Once they had exchanged a few pleasantries, the tailor signaled for him to step into the booth at the rear of the store. It smelled of turpentine and an odor K. could not quite identify. The booth was black as pitch. A bare bulb hung from a chain just above his head, but there was no pull cord, and the one window had been blocked out with an assortment of severed coat sleeves. The tailor told K. to strip and stand still. He closed his eyes. In the dark, all he could hear was the dreadful snipping of scissors.

EVIDENCE

Dressed in a blue suit which he had just picked up from the tailor, and wearing a false mustache which he had fixed to his upper lip with spirit gum, K. slipped through the metal detectors, made his way down the corridor, and snuck into the court room, where his trial was already proceeding in his absence. Lawyers opened briefcases and rifled the pages of their legal pads. Witnesses shuffled to the stand and delivered their testimony. But for all the moving lips, the banging gavel and the swishing black robes, K. heard nothing but the steady typing of the court stenographer. She was pretty, perhaps thirty-five, and her slender fingers moved with such dizzying celerity that they struck him as a kind of hectic calm. Just as he began to back his way out of the courtroom, she turned and looked at him. Everything went on as before, except that when she stood from her swivel chair, her red mouth turning up slightly at the corners, she unbuttoned her blouse and opened it to his gaze. What Joseph K. saw could not easily be described. His face turned pale. There, buried in the folds of her shirt, white and enormous, lay the irrefutable evidence that had so long been kept from him.

RESEARCH

At the windowpane in front of K.'s desk, snow was falling. It fell from clouds that looked like tangled gauze, and it fell on ditches and rooftops, whirling down to dapple the faces of the local statues and deposit its lucent dust on their shoulders. As snow kept accumulating on the glass and in the eaves, K. closed, one by one, the open windows on his computer—karaoke lyrics and fondue recipes, articles about the fate of the pangolins and the sordid previous lives of the Dalia Lama—until only the search engine was left. Letter by letter, he typed the familiar words "Joseph K." What else did the authorities know about him? He took a deep breath while the hard drive cogitated. The snow churned and eddied at the pane. Seconds passed. He expected to find the usual results—birth records, a list of old telephone numbers and addresses, perhaps an embarrassing Facebook photograph that he had since deleted—but what he found instead unsettled him. In place of data, tech logos, or advertisements, was simply a blank screen, empty as a winter field covered in snow. Outside, the actual snow would fall till morning, flake after flake like the details of his life, rising on the cold air briefly, then spiraling nowhere. Was this all there was? K. stared at the courthouse from his snow-blind window, then at the white screen. He had found nothing. A cursor blinked there, where his name had been.

The Reason

The heart has reasons, Pascal said, which reason
knows nothing of. But I think we know the reason.

The man combs his dark hair and trims his beard,
but the woman who swipes left still has a reason.

The plane lost altitude and smacked a mountain?
Check the black box for the official reason.

He said he'd left his three kids at the shelter
when he lost his job, and clung hard to the reason.

If the twister killed the whole congregation
at Wednesday service, well, isn't God the reason?

Winning the war at the cost of all his men:
yes, that was a calculus the general could reason.

Another late-night jag, the waking with my cheek
on the same cold tile, the exonerating reason—

Morri, I ask the mirror, *why all these dark lines?*
I'm just a rhyme, he says. *You are the reason.*

Twilight

IDYLL

The sun is a streak of peach across the lake,
moon a gown of gauze caught in the trees.
Between the spigot and the garden rake
the spider spins its tenuous trapeze.

REFUTATION AT DAWN

Truth is on hold. Philosophers, take note:
a barn dissolves into the muffling mist.
The solid world slips off on Charon's boat
to vex the dreams of the materialist.

ALPHA AND OMEGA

To make the morning is to unmake night,
whatever else one chooses to believe.
It's darkness that first said Let There Be Light:
the great creator with Nothing up its sleeve.

PERILS OF WISDOM

Though honeybees retreat into the hive
and lilies' throats constrict at close of day,
the best of fates is still to be alive
for all the honeyed words the ancients say.

INTERLUDE

No sound for miles. Not even a hint of wind.
The swing sets in the local park are still.
It's like the quiet calm at supper's end
shortly before the waiter brings the bill.

HOROSCOPE

At dawn and dusk the future meets the past.
The stars, for all they govern, irk the mind—
those glittering dice the universe has cast
on the empty baize by which they are defined.

COMPOSITION IN GRAY

Have twilit meanings spun between the lines
not always been the subject of the text?
The maker gets snared in his own designs:
from word to world, one sentence to the next.

Beginning

That day God spun the wind to tick time forward.
It teased gold from the leaf, flung spores and seeds.
The beasts' fur billowed. A long-legged shorebird
swung its hunger above a froth of reeds.

The restless trees leaned—bent—all pitch and wring.
Not yet the serpent's tryst in the grass. Not yet
Abel slain in the field, the Lord's voice calling.
Still, earth toiled at its purposes: the fret

and seethe of larvae started in the mud.
Rain scoured the stone to spill its mineral dust.
Straight rivers cut their convoluted maze.

And when the vole twitched in the marsh hawk's gaze
God turned away from that place of moth and rust
as wings beat toward the heaven of the blood.

The Road

1.

I met the past
        on a country road

out where the poor
        bury their dead

it was after dark
        the house I sought

wore the mist
        like an overcoat

where are you going
        he said to me

the briar bush
        the house the lea

the stars too all
        are fugitive

the backward look
        is how you live

2.

So I followed him
           breath on the air

trailed behind me
           like despair

and I could hear
           those several winds

that helped the means
           achieve the ends

from the fool's oath
           to the wise decree

to the proud tower
           to the gallows tree

I asked him for
           his name he said

I am the wormwood
           the bitter bread

3.

The past grinned
        to show me all

the raftered bones
        that built the fall

the promises
        that led to grief

like tent worms
        on a locust leaf

those dividends
        that drove the lash

and sunk the soldier's
        boots in ash

the things I saw there
        struck me dumb

my own town burned
        his kingdom come

4.

He held midnight
                in his hands

the dark was his
                to give commands

he conjured up
                the Spanish fleet

that bore abroad
                the spirochete

Hiroshima
                as it stood before

the blind breach
                at the atom's core

plant your shovel
                deep in lime

he said *you'll prize*
                some founding crime

5.

His hand unlocked
        the masks I'd worn

to hide myself
        since I was born

the awkward kid
        without a cent

at twenty-five
        turned arrogant

the drunk who stared
        in an empty cup

and the rake who turned
        his collar up

but when I asked
        which one was me

no turn of phrase
        would twist the key

6.

I said to him
              I've had enough

he reached and grabbed me
                                   by the scruff

boy he said
              though you're still here

with every breath
              you disappear

the future's just
              a tightening noose

and no one
              can snatch you loose

I am your compass
                   your north star

I am the nothing
              that you are

7.

I looked ahead
        and traveled on

three times a rooster
        signaled dawn

the house I sought
        was a few steps more

my shadow stretched
        to the front door

the road behind
        seemed like a spool

of thread unraveled
        by a fool

then someone said
        you've found the place

it was his voice
        it was my face

After Lorca

Pero no son los muertos los que bailan.
—*Federico García Lorca*

I'm sure there are no dancers among the dead,
despite the red leaves spinning from the tree.
Heaven and hell both lie in the same bed.

Though at the end, in the mind, one trails the thread
of breath in slow steps, without company,
I'm sure there are no dancers among the dead.

For all the wings, or tongues of fire, ahead,
nothing will have something to do to me.
Heaven and hell both lie in the same bed.

The mountain looms where flesh can never tread.
Though spirit reels and staggers on the scree,
I'm sure it is no dancer. Among the dead,

who fail to stir for what the prophets said,
a windless flake of ash is enough to see
heaven and hell both lie. In the same bed

God and His absence stretch out feet to head,
tugging their blanket for eternity.
I'm sure there are no dancers among the dead.
Heaven and hell both lie in the same bed.

Cape Cod Evening

Edward Hopper, oil on canvas, 30×40 in.

The way she folds her arms across
her waist while evening closes in

as though she bears some private loss
she'll have to grieve alone again,

the way he reaches out to call
the dog that will not come, that stands

in deep grass at the edge of fall
and turns away from his commands—

even the way the house looks bare,
its windows giving on to no

bland views of couch or Frigidaire
or any comforts we might know,

or the way shadows pool around
those trees which seem to vanish fast,

burrowing root-hairs in the ground
like something buried in the past—

makes us believe they won't last long,
this couple painted years ago.

Autumn is one way things went wrong.
The sallow grass awaits the snow.

III.

3.

Summer seems cradled in an oyster shell
that time pries open with a shucking knife.
The realtor next door has new shares to sell.
He grew up near your town. He knows your wife.

You tell him you grew up here in a way,
collecting shells and swimming in the creek.
A cloud has turned the sky gunmetal gray.
You ask about the forecast for the week

but get no answer. It rains here every year.
Once, when you were twelve, it rained for days,
and you read Tolkien novels in the bed

while your dad paced the rec room with a beer,
tracing his thumb on the pool table's baize.
It's calm now, but it's storming in your head.

4.

The last thirty-five years stretch out of reach
like a kite string raveling out in summer winds.
At dawn the low sun ripens like a peach.
Your joints ache, like a diver's with the bends.

You spent last night out drinking on the deck
with your neighbor, a chiropractor from Fort Wayne,
then woke with a fishing net around your neck.
Your head throbs to the breakers' far refrain.

Each evening ends up pretty much like this.
The sea stacks up the days, you knock them down
till they're just a few postcards, souvenirs,

or lies you swap with strangers over beers.
Sunrise puts on the colors of a clown.
You stumble toward the dock to take a piss.

5.

You run five miles past tourist shops that sell
your childhood: t-shirts, hermit crabs, shark teeth.
Summers seem fine at first, until the smell
prompts you to look and see what's underneath—

cut to the queasy mornings, quarrels, rain,
the tilt-a-whirl operator's crooked smile.
Each dawn your eyes fix on the water stain
like a Rorschach blot across the ceiling tile

until you find the strength to lace your shoes.
But once you're out here jogging on the strand
you're persuaded by the morning's garish sprawl,

the Ferris wheel looming above the sand
and the wind tumbling over a child's beach ball.
On the sea a lone cloud darkens like a bruise.

6.

Painted sand dollars at fifteen dollars each.
The boardwalk's whiff of hot dogs and cheap beer.
A shuttered surf shop where they used to teach
out-of-towners to kayak past the pier.

Horizons stretched flat as a straight-edge razor,
above which doze the same thick plumes of cloud.
Bicycle cop, right hand perched on his Taser.
The pool. No cursing. Diving not allowed.

When did your parents first start taking you
here, and why did they come back every summer?
And won't your kids be asking the same thing

in ten years? Won't the answers still be true?
You lean in the salt wind to feel the sting.
With every gust your face keeps getting number.

7.

The fortune tellers don't have much to tell:
you met a girl in school and married her,
then hunkered down, a diver in a bell.
The years from then to now are just a blur.

You glimpse her leaning out on the deck rail
and close your eyes. She's still the girl you knew,
isn't she? Brown hair. Willowy and pale.
Sometimes you wonder what she thinks of you.

As for the future, it'll look much like this,
except you'll both be older, and she'll seem
reserved somehow, more distant, like she keeps

a secret to outlast your carelessness.
This afternoon you'll watch her as she sleeps
and reach for her, then leave her to her dream.

8.

A radio stammers on the edge of speech.
Thunder is clearing its throat above the sea.
The sun looks pale, like it's been soaked in bleach
where it hangs from the frond of a palmetto tree.

Last night was quiet till you raised your voice.
Your wife shushed you and wrinkled up her face
because, she said, you might wake up the boys,
then locked herself in the bedroom just in case.

Now things are pleasant, and the kids look fine,
digging their heels in mud when the waves retreat.
Your wife reads a paperback in a rusted chair

while you sip from a plastic Solo cup of wine.
You think to apologize, but you don't dare.
Another wave collapses at your feet.

9.

While a half-moon flicks its ash into the sand
you sit in a rocking chair and watch the breeze
wrinkle the inlet, half-drunk and suntanned
with a map of Myrtle Beach across your knees.

What will it be today, you ask: putt-putt
or a day trip out to Ripley's Believe It or Not?
Your wife scowls at you. A screen door slams shut.
It's nine o'clock in the morning and too hot.

Your father used to herd you to the car
on some grim errand, then, in the name of fun,
head to the amusement park and let you ride,

turning you into the father that you are.
You think of him, his hand blocking the sun,
thrilled just to hear the bumper cars collide.

10.

This isn't how it was when you were ten—
face down in a sand dune with a blistered back
at eleven a.m. You don't know where you've been.
A bar. Six bourbon shots. Beer. Fade to black.

You walk the quarter mile back to the house
trailing a busted flip-flop from your heel
to hear your wife, exhausted, fume and grouse
while you try to play it off like no big deal.

As you pass the pier, a woman looks at you.
Somebody that you met the night before?
The light chews at your eyes. Your head's on fire.

If you don't remember it, you're not a liar,
you think the minute you walk through the door.
The story you tell isn't honest. But it's true.

11.

Shirtless, you wade waist deep into the ocean
while your seven-year-old rides a boogey board.
He wants to go out deep past the commotion.
You say one minute, but by then you're bored.

Your own father once took you on his shoulders
out past the tideline where the sea was calm.
You squint back at the beach. The sun smolders,
stuck like a Frisbee in some ragged palm.

Later, you'll put your feet up, watch TV
in one of a dozen houses that you've rented
over the years, and think *I'm not my father.*

You see him, son in his arms, breasting the sea
like parenthood was something he invented.
After the next wave, you say. But you won't bother.

12.

The minute hand has inched past the hour hand.
Butch + Amanda banged here 2016,
scrawled in a Port-O-John out past the strand,
reminds you no one's hands are ever clean

no matter how much soap they lather on.
The moon's a seashell on some motel sign,
a tinsel decoration for the dawn;
sun bobs like a cork on the horizon line.

You run to sweat the night out of your pores
past houses lined like rows of old mistakes
that greet you every morning when you rise;

the repetition still won't make you wise
no matter all the breaths or miles it takes
to find the address you'll recognize as yours.

13.

On the town hall clock, now subsides to then.
You run to convince yourself it's just the summer.
The realtor from next door asks where you've been,
smiling and waving at you from his Hummer.

You slept the last two nights at the Island Dunes
Motel in Surfside. There's an ice machine
and a pool with a diving board. You watch cartoons
all day in your pajamas like a teen.

You think of who you were eight years ago.
Modest. Almost successful. Calm. Sincere.
You thought you held the future in your hands,

strolling the pier in swim trunks and Ray-Bans.
Whatever happened to you happened slow.
The window unit drones. You crack a beer.

14.

The morning smells of trash and suntan lotion,
but it's too late to dwell on imperfections.
You run out past the condos by the ocean,
past cheap rides and kiosks that sell confections

and stores with souvenir shot glasses on a shelf.
Reflected in the window, you're your dad
for a moment, then a stranger, then yourself.
The whole thing seems more ridiculous than sad.

You stare at an umber smutch beyond the pier.
A seagull, hefting a French fry in its beak,
struts in the sand beside a garbage bin.

It's always been this summer, every year.
The salt wind off the sea still chafes your cheek.
You'll head back home. The waves keep coming in.

The Sentence

He sat at the desk across from his reflection
watching him where it hung above the mantel

and studied the hand there writing what he wrote,
something about the ocean in midsummer

when he was a child, the glint, the flecks of spume
tossed up where breakers thundered on the rocks;

the truth was a sentence they composed together
for no one else but the quiet of the house:

the tide he dreamt and the one he could remember,
subject and verb and the sun-touched swells they made

of the past itself now blended with invention,
his left hand moving the right hand in the mirror

and time a distance in the room between them,
spread out there like a childhood shore, where waves

broke on the sand and retreated to the green sea.

ACKNOWLEDGMENTS

Thanks to the following publications, where many of these poems first appeared:

Alabama Literary Review: "Burning the Leaves," "*Cape Cod Evening*," "The Road," "Search," and "Twilight"; *American Journal of Poetry*: "House of Correction" and "The Sentence"; *Antioch Review*: "Near the Summer Pavilion"; *The Book of Life (21st Editions)*: "Beginning"; *Hopkins Review*: "House Fire at the Sea" and "The Sentence"; *Literary Matters*: "Grievance," "Mileage," "The Reason," and "Time"; *The New Criterion*: "The Sentence," "Triumph of the New," and "Witness"; *Quarterly West*: "If Shakespeare"; *Smartish Pace*: "The Trial"; and *Yale Review*: "Shadow."

"House Fire at the Sea" is dedicated to Sarah Creech. "Witness" is dedicated to Michael Shewmaker. "The Trial" is dedicated to Rick Pryll and Holly Spruck. "Grievance" is dedicated to Joshua Mehigan. "Near the Summer Pavilion" is dedicated to my father.

Special thanks to Michael Shewmaker, Joseph Harrison, Chris Forhan, Julie Funderburk, Michael Kobre, and Sarah Creech for their advice, suggestions, and encouragement.

NOTES

"The Sentence" (p. 5): the final line borrows from the Talmud (Yevamot 97a).

"The Sentence" (p. 33): In November 1933, Osip Mandelstam wrote his famous "Stalin Epigram," in which he describes Stalin's mustache as cockroaches running across the dictator's lip. For this poem, Mandelstam was arrested and interrogated, then banished to Voronezh, and finally sentenced to hard labor in a gulag. He died of hunger and cold in a transit camp in 1938. "The Sentence" owes a debt to Nadezhda Mandelstam's memoir *Hope Against Hope*.

"If Shakespeare" (p. 41): The poem takes its title and central premise from Virginia Woolf's essay "If Shakespeare Had a Sister."

"Perils of Wisdom" (p. 52): W. B. Yeats, paraphrasing a passage from Sophocles' *Oedipus at Colonus*:

> Never to have lived is best, ancient writers say;
> Never to have drawn the breath of life, never to have looked into the eye of day;
> The second best's a gay goodnight and quickly turn away.
> —W. B. Yeats, "A Man Young and Old"

"Beginning" (p. 56): The line "God turned away from that place of moth and rust" references Matthew 16: 19–20.

"The Road" (p. 57): line 2 of section 3 alludes to *Paradise Lost,* Book 4, lines 519–20.

"After Lorca" (p. 64): The line "I'm sure there are no dancers among the dead" is from Lorca's poem "Danza de la muerte," translated by Greg Simon and Steven White (Federico García Lorca: Collected Poems, revised edition, with an introduction and notes by Christopher Maurer. New York: FSG, 1991).

"Near the Summer Pavilion" (p. 69): The line "you hear the mermaids singing each to each" borrows from T. S. Eliot's "The Love Song of J. Alfred Prufrock," line 124. The poem owes a debt to John Cheever's "The Swimmer."

Printed in the USA
CPSIA information can be obtained
at www.ICGtesting.com
LVHW091227151223
766489LV00004B/454